MW01251603

Written in Pen

My name is Emmerson Grin and I write original excerpts/quotes, typically in black gel pen.

ISBN: 978-1-365-24985-3

Published by: Paige McDaniel

Emmerson Grin

Written in Pen

This is dedicated to everyone I've ever written about, and everyone who will never know the words I have written in their name.
May you find happiness.

— E. Grin

Emmerson Grin

Deep Thinking

Written in Pen

"I don't ever find myself listening to those who say, 'Don't swim across oceans for people who wouldn't step over a puddle for you,' because what a stupid saying that is. I feel that if it means enough to you, you should swim the oceans, and cross the lands, because even if there's no pot of gold at the end of your long journey, you still got to experience new things, and you get to say you did it all for something that meant a lot to you, even if it didn't end up being there. It doesn't matter what's at the end of the race, it's all in the effort you put in to get there."

— E. Grin

Emmerson Grin

"It sucks, doesn't it?"

"Huh?"

"Feeling like the most beautiful rainbow in the world while loving a color-blind man."

— E. Grin

Written in Pen

"I'm sorry," He admitted, not being able to look at me.

"No," I say, "I knew it'd end. No reason to apologize."

"But if you knew it'd end, why'd you let yourself get hurt?"

"Because," I told him, "even if I know my favorite song will eventually end, that won't stop me from enjoying it."

— E. Grin

Emmerson Grin

"When I first fell for your eyes, I figured it was because they
reminded me of the way sunlight reflects of the ocean,
but months pass us by while I find myself walking on the shore,
trying to figure out why the ocean is my favorite view, and I see
the sunlight reflecting off the water, as if your eyes were my
favorite view, like maybe the ocean means nothing to me, and
you're the only reason I ever visit the sandy sea-side."

— E. Grin

"He's as glorious as all the constellations, galaxies, and the moon, but even the moon has a dark side."

— E. Grin

He was the song I've always tried to sing, but I was never in key."

— E. Grin

Written in Pen

"You gave me a feeling that I can't rewind, and the end credits have been rolling for months now, but I cannot stop replaying a scene in my head that never existed in the first place."

— E. Grin

Emmerson Grin

"You act as my sanity and losing you would mean losing my mind."

— E. Grin

Written in Pen

"What color would you use to describe him?" She asks me, tapping her pen on her desk.

"Color?" I ask, "What's that got to do with anything?"

In a monotone voice she tells me, "Just give it a go."

"Yeah, okay," I stall, sighing, "Grey. I think grey is a good color to describe him."

"And why's that?"

I swallow, looking at the ground, almost wanting to smile, but deciding to avoid the thought.

"Because," I begin, "he had a dark side. He was depressing and dark and mysterious, all the while he was also bright, and knew just how to make me smile. His dark side never compared to his elegant side, but somehow I still found comfort in loving his hidden corners, like maybe I longed to live in the shadows, as long as they were his."

— E. Grin

Emmerson Grin

"What do you feel?"

"I don't," I tell, "I don't feel."

"Why's that?"

I tap my fingers against the desk in front of me, "Because what we feel is what we've chosen to believe."

"And what do you believe in?"

I smile sarcastically, "I don't believe in anything."

— E. Grin

"Tragedy isn't loving the wrong person thinking they are the right, but it is loving the right person and thinking they are the wrong."

— E. Grin

Emmerson Grin

This is how I put relationships:
If you loved one man, but you fell for another, you never loved
the first. Choose the second one you've fallen for.

— E. Grin

Written in Pen

"His light reflected off me, as if I was the Moon and he was the Sun, but as soon as he left, I was left in the dark, so the darkness I became."

— E. Grin

"You're art," I tell him suddenly.

"Why do you think that?" He asks, looking over at me.

"You remind me of a painting that maybe no one understands," I inform, "a really beautiful painting that everyone seems to long for, but can't find the meaning."

"Oh," He sighs.

"And," I interrupt his moping, "maybe many don't understand you now, but that doesn't mean someone else won't walk up to you and understand every brush stroke."

— E. Grin

"Rainbows are illusions of refracted light, making you see something that isn't there, and I think that's just what our love was; an illusion."

— E. Grin

Emmerson Grin

"You're either the artist or the art."

— E. Grin

Written in Pen

"I feel useless," He says to me.

"Why so?"

"I mean think about it," He speaks, "this Universe holds so many galaxies, planets, and stars. Plus, what's to say there isn't any other life? I'm basically a speck of dust."

"But you hold more meaning than any other speck of dust."

"But I'm also tiny compared to everything else."

"Well," I smile, "so are the stars, from a distance."

"What are you saying?" He asks.

"I'm saying that you're a star, and anyone who says otherwise just isn't close enough."

— E. Grin

Emmerson Grin

"Time was killing me before I could kill it, and soon enough I
became a ticking time-bomb with only seconds to spare."

— E. Grin

Written in Pen

"There's a flame inside us all," He tells me, playing with his black lighter.

He flicks the BIC on, igniting it.

Continuing, he says, "The fire represents our life, our thoughts."

His eyes focus on the bright light, letting it consume his words.

"And it'll either blow out too soon, or set one on fire completely."

I smile a sad smile, "Let's hope I don't burn alive."

"Yeah," He begins, "and let's hope I don't fade away."

— E. Grin

Emmerson Grin

"I like the stars," I tell him.

He shoots a small smile, "I know."

"They inspire me, you know?"

"Yes," He laughs, "I know."

"But, get this," I throw.

"What?"

"They, the stars themselves, don't inspire me."

"Hmm?"

"It's who makes me curious about those stars," I say, "It's the one who gave me the courage to look up at the sky and wonder."

"And who would that be?"

I look over at him, "You."

— E. Grin

Written in Pen

"You're not the girl of my dreams," He said, and I was ready to become saddened, but he continued, "You're more real."

— E. Grin

Emmerson Grin

"I fell in love with my sadness," I tell the sky, "but it's not like I want to be sad."

I lie down on the concrete below me, letting myself star gaze as the night grows darker.

"As dark as it sounds, though," I give a laugh, "sadness was the only thing that stuck by my side while everyone else left."

I trace the darkness with my eyes, wishing on every shooting star I could find.

"I almost had no choice but to bond with what was left behind. All I wanted was a friend, and I got left with sorrow."

— E. Grin

Written in Pen

"You're an artist," I tell him.

"How so?"

"You paint a smile on every face you come across," I say, "but there's always a twist with artists."

"What's my twist?"

"You never paint a smile on yourself."

— E. Grin

Emmerson Grin

A Love as Deep as the Sea

Written in Pen

"I've fallen
in love with
adventures,

so I begin to wonder,

if that's why
I've fallen for you."

— E. Grin

Emmerson Grin

"He was a story that never hit the paper and his eyes were paintings that never hit the canvas."

— E. Grin

Written in Pen

"Someone once told me that I'd never be able to love unless I learned to love myself, but I loved him so much that I forgot what hating myself felt like."

— E. Grin

Emmerson Grin

"Hey," My friend greets, but I only give a shy smile in reply.

"What's up?" She asks, nodding her head towards my notebook.

"Just finished writing," I tell, tapping my pen against the grey leather that jacketed the paper.

"You haven't been yourself lately."

I almost laugh, but instead I feel a tear fall from my left eye.

"Guess not," I shrug.

"Why are you crying?" She worries, leaning into me with tissues.

"I guess," I start, "I guess I cry when someone starts to realize I'm not okay."

— E. Grin

Written in Pen

Do you ever love someone so much it feels like your heart rebreaks itself every day just to feel something other than that love?

— E. Grin

Emmerson Grin

"People often say they love the rain because it drowns out their thoughts, or lets them know that they're not the only ones crying, but to me, to me it lets me know that even an existence as empty as the sky can still feel something; lets me know that I'll get there some day."

— E. Grin

Written in Pen

"I don't play with fire but I'd burn for you."

— E. Grin

Emmerson Grin

"I had always imagined adventures as 3am walks through a canyon, or maybe a late night drive around downtown, but then I met you and I've now realized how an adventure could be anything, even a person."

— E. Grin

Written in Pen

"This would be easier if I didn't let myself get attached," I say to him.

"No," He sighs, "I shouldn't have let you."

"You have no control over who gets attached to you or not."

"I do," He glares.

"Shut up," I tell, "I'm trying to leave you and you're distracting me."

He smiles a very weak smile, "No, you're running away from something that you don't understand."

"So," I look over at him, "make me understand and I won't have to run."

— E. Grin

Emmerson Grin

"Staring at the old pictures of you I've been too scared to delete, I begin to wonder if I'd see them at 1am, drunk off the leftovers of our love, and I wonder if I'd call you, and I wonder if you'd be high off the broken pieces of my heart, and I wonder if you'd answer."

— E. Grin

Written in Pen

"Your happiness is my first priority," I tell, "Even if-"

"Even if what?" He growls, "Are you gonna feed me romantic slurs about how you want me to be happy without you?"

"I-"

He cuts me off once again, "And what if you're my happiness? What if me happy means you sticking by my side?"

I sigh deeply, "Then you should consider sticking by mine."

— E. Grin

Emmerson Grin

"If you love me, let me go," He tells me, trying to loosen my grip on his hand.

"No."

"No?"

"No," I firmly say for a second time.

"Why not? Do you not love me?"

I roll my eyes, "I do, I do love you with all of my heart, but that's just it."

"What?" He questions.

"You don't let the one you love walk out of your life. When you love someone or something, you fight for them, even if you know you'll lose, because in the end, if you've won, it's all worth the war you fought."

— E. Grin

Written in Pen

"His words were dry, like a desert, and her mind was as unexplored as a rain forest. They intertwined their fingers, balancing each other out in a way of excellence, like maybe she was his rain and he was her drought, like maybe their galaxies touched and created the Earth; a balance between droughts and floods."

— E. Grin

Emmerson Grin

"He was a galaxy while I was only a star, but hey, stars burn bright, too."

— E. Grin

Written in Pen

"He was the heat, she was the cold, and together, they were a storm."

— E. Grin

Emmerson Grin

"He wondered why he was never good with words, but all along he was the poetry and never the poet."

— E. Grin

Written in Pen

"He was the type of boy you saw in the dumpsters behind an art museum, looking for abandoned art, and I suppose that's how he'll find himself, because I have never seen such an imperfect masterpiece in my life."

— E. Grin

Emmerson Grin

"He was magnificent, and there's no doubt in saying he fascinated me, but it was in a way where I'd rather stare at him than any brightly lit, night sky. It was in a way where I'd rather read him than any self-provoking book. He was someone who I would spend my life figuring out if it meant I got to be in his presence at all, and that'd be the best part; being there for him, even if I was struggling."

— E. Grin

Written in Pen

"Why?" He asked me stubbornly, as if I'd done something wrong.

"Why what?"

"Why do you still love me?"

I was taken back by his question, needing to take a deep breath before I could answer.

"Well," I bite, "maybe it's the way your hair falls after a long day, or how you speak-"

"No," He cuts me off, "no jokes. Tell me why."

I sigh, "Maybe I still love you because a love as real as I gave you, it doesn't leave, even if the end credits rolled by months ago."

"Okay," He simply says.

I smile a sad smile, "Think of it as the scene every few people wait for after the credits, you just have to wait."

— E. Grin

Emmerson Grin

"He watched the constellations envelope her thoughts, making her tears shooting stars and her laugh as contagious as her love for the night sky."

— E. Grin

Written in Pen

"I am nothing," He sighs, his lip nearly quivering.

"Don't say that," I say, "It's not true."

Seeing him hurt made me hurt, and I'm glad I didn't have to lie to make him feel better. I am telling the truth, and that's the best part.

"But-"

I cut him off, "No, don't start."

"You don't understand," He argues.

"No, you don't understand," I bark, "because when I look at you, I see someone with potential, and a purpose. You are an art museum full of the most beautiful masterpieces, and everyone who thinks otherwise, they've just got their eyes closed."

— E. Grin

Emmerson Grin

"You're so fascinated with something as simple as the sky, or the moon," He says, "Why do you love the simple things in life when you hold so much more depth?"

I give a laugh, "Have you looked at yourself in the mirror lately?"

His furrowed eyebrows tell me he has no idea what I'm saying.

"You're the most complicated thing I have ever interacted with," I smile, "and I am so fascinated with you, much more than I am with the 'simple sky.'"

— E. Grin

Written in Pen

"You remind me of the ocean," I say.

"And why's that?"

"Only five percent of the ocean is discovered," I begin, "but nothing is stopping anyone from trying to solve the mysteries the big blue holds."

"Your point?"

"Who says anyone is stopping me from solving you?"

— E. Grin

Emmerson Grin

"You must really love the stars." He says, watching as I gaze up at the sky full of unfulfilled wishes.

"You could say that."

"Would there be anything else to say about it?"

"I mean, take a look," I tell, "These stars aren't just some glowing blobs. I've got this feeling that they're made up of every failed wish, and every declined fairy tale."

He nods his head, looking over at my fascination with the sky.

"A lot of my wishes were about you," I whisper.

"What's that got to do with anything?"

"They all failed," I sigh, "so, doesn't that make you the sky?"

— E. Grin

Written in Pen

"He lies awake, wondering if her love was true, and he knows he shouldn't doubt her, but that boy has never felt something as genuine as her love in his life."

— E. Grin

Emmerson Grin

"You look nice," I say, "but more like art."

"Hmm?"

"You look more like art than nice, in my opinion."

He furrows his eyebrows, "What's that supposed to mean?"

"It means that if we were in a room full of art," I smile, "you'd be my favorite piece."

— E. Grin

Spilled Ink

Emmerson Grin

"Why are you leaving?"

He looks over his shoulder at me, "Because I love you."

"No," I say, "that's not how it works."

He sighs in my direction, waiting for an explanation.

"You leave someone because you don't love someone, not because you do."

His eyes begin to water, "Then maybe I don't."

— E. Grin

"I loved you," He admits, avoiding eye contact.

I sniffle, making it barely noticeable, "Then why can't you look at me?"

He takes a deep breath, looking away once again.

"Hmm?" I push.

"Because," He stalls, "because I think I still do."

— E. Grin

Emmerson Grin

"What's wrong?" He asks, watching as my mood had dropped just moments before.

"What? Nothing," I assure, trying to believe my own lie.

Which, I wasn't entirely lying, because in some twisted way, nothing was actually wrong, it was just wrong to me.

"Lies."

"Nothing is wrong," I snap, "drop it."

"Ha-ha no."

My eyes roll as I get up, grabbing my leather jacket from the seat I had been sitting in.

"I'm going to go home, and if the world starts being torn apart piece by piece, the first call I'd make would be to you."

He furrows his eyebrows, "There's something wrong with that?"

"Yes," I nod, "because the line would be dead, since you'd be on the phone with someone else."

— E. Grin

Written in Pen

"Have you ever wanted to be loved?" He asks me, attempting to make eye contact with me, but I look away.

"Yes," I reply.

"Then why did you run from it?"

I sigh, "It's one of those feelings."

Confused, he questions what I mean.

"One of those feelings where you're running from the boy you like in a game of tag on the playground back in third grade. Where you're running, giggling like the small child you are, but you want to stop. You want to stop running to see what would happen if he caught up to you, but you know you'd lose the game if you slowed, so your legs continue moving."

I look at my hands, still avoiding his eye contact.

"I wanted to stop," I whisper, "I wanted to stop running just to see what would happen if love caught up to me, but my instincts told me someone was chasing me, so I only sped up. I didn't want to lose the game of tag."

— E. Grin

Emmerson Grin

"He became my sanity in a world full of the insane, and losing him would mean losing my mind."

— E. Grin

Written in Pen

"Your eyes are the sea and tonight I'm drowning."

— E. Grin

Emmerson Grin

"He had the stars in the palm of his hand, but all he seemed to see was a few reflections, and that said a lot about how he saw himself."

— E. Grin

Written in Pen

"Hey," He says to me, but I ignore it.

"Um… Hello?" He waves his hand in front my face, and I roll my eyes. He huffs, rolling his, too.

"Are we playing the quiet game? If so, I've already lost so you can speak now."

I laugh to myself, making it only a little audible, but it still makes him annoyed.

"What'd I do this time?" He whines.

I look him straight in the eyes, "You pushed a loyal person to the point where they no longer care."

He goes silent, not daring to speak.

"See, now I've lost at the quiet game, yet another game of yours I'm the loser of."

— E. Grin

Emmerson Grin

"He'll drink until he discovers she won't be at the bottom of the whiskey bottle, and instead it will appear empty just like his heart."

— E. Grin

Written in Pen

"Did you love him?"

"Yes."

"Did he love you back?"

"Sometimes."

— E. Grin

Emmerson Grin

"Someday," He tells her, "you'll learn to hate me, and as you dig up that long overdue hatred, you'll also find peace; peace in yourself, because while loving me may be the adventure you've been searching for all this time," He pauses, "you've lost your trail, and you need to be on the right track to get to your destination, and darling, your destination is not me."

— E. Grin

Written in Pen

"You need to go home," My friend says, watching me down whatever was left in my red solo cup.

I laughed for a second, before wiping my eyes.

"What's so funny?" She snaps.

"Nothing," I giggle, "nothing."

"Okay, go home."

I burst out laughing again.

"Seriously!" She yells, "Why?"

"Well, miss loud voice," I cover my mouth to keep from laughing once again, "my home doesn't want me there."

— E. Grin

Emmerson Grin

"I sat there, looking for a hint of love for me left in those eyes, but then I laughed to myself, because, well, you can't find something that was never there in the first place."

— E. Grin

Written in Pen

"His words were toxic and I slowly became a wasteland."

— E. Grin

Emmerson Grin

"What do you believe in?" He asks, stirring his water with the straw.

"I mean, define what you're asking."

"Um," He stalls, "like, God, soulmates, things like that."

"I don't exactly believe in God," I say, "and as for soulmates, I used to."

"Used to? Did the guy before me ruin your life or something?" He laughs.

I give a weak laugh as the memories come flooding back, "Yeah, or something."

— E. Grin

Written in Pen

"Reality has become an ocean where I no longer know how to swim, and everyone around me seems to be paddling along just fine."

— E. Grin

Emmerson Grin

"I began loving you with every piece of me, and that's just what they were; tiny, broken pieces."

— E. Grin

Written in Pen

"When you left, there were parts of me that wanted to tell you how much I loved you so you would stay, but your words triggered another part of me which reminded me that a re-lit cigarette will never taste the same, so I let you go, and I let our flame blow out with ease."

— E. Grin

Emmerson Grin

"You'll find another," He says to me, "It'll get better."

I shake my head, "No, you don't understand."

"I do."

"No," I exclaim, "you don't!"

"Look," He goes, "I really don't have time for this conversation."

"Then make time, because what I have with you, I don't want with anyone else."

— E. Grin

Written in Pen

"Why should I stay?" He asks, not looking in my direction.

My eyes have been watering, "Because I care."

He doesn't make a sound, as if silently signaling for me to go on.

"You taught me how to shine in a world of glow sticks, and you taught me how to love myself even if no one else would."

A tear falls from his eye as he moves his head, gazing down at his feet.

"I care about you," I speak, "and if that's not enough, then maybe you're right. Maybe it's time you go."

— E. Grin

Emmerson Grin

"I began chasing shooting stars in hopes they'd give me a chance to fall out of love with the boy who only wanted still constellations."

— E. Grin

Written in Pen

"He represented every heartbreak, every tear, and every piece of glass she ever shattered, but no matter the pain or guilt she felt towards his meaning, the girl couldn't take her eyes off him, like maybe he was another chance for her to gain forgiveness, or maybe he was another shot at love."

— E. Grin

Emmerson Grin

"I used to take my coffee black as night but, after him, I began adding sugar and cream, as if he was enough bitterness to wake me up for a lifetime."

— E. Grin

Written in Pen

"Why'd you give up on me?" He asks.

I sigh, "It's not that I gave up on you, yourself, I just gave up on figuring you out."

He looks at me, slightly saddened, "And why's that?"

"Because," I start, "some things are meant to be left as mysteries."

— E. Grin

Emmerson Grin

"Why does it hurt?"

I look up at the lady who I've been speaking to for weeks now.

"Because I said goodbye," I tell her.

"To who?"

"To the person who worked up enough courage to say hello."

— E. Grin

Written in Pen

"Do you think we could've made it?" I ask him.

He looks over at me, his arm still around my shoulders.

"Hi," He says.

I nod back and try to continue walking, but he stops me.

"I don't get a 'hello?'"

I shake my head no, trying to maintain a cheeky, sarcastic smile.

"Why don't I get a greeting? Come on," He sighs.

I look up at him with acid-filled eyes, "No, you don't get a stupid greeting, you wanna know why? Because I'm quite terrified that it'll come out as an, 'I still love you even though you shattered my heart to pieces,' instead of a simple, 'hello.'"

And with that, I walk away.

— E. Grin

Emmerson Grin

"Yes," He goes, "I think we could've made it, even if it was us against the world."

"But now it's you against me," I sigh.

"Never in a million years would it be us against each other. Love just timed us wrong."

"Wouldn't it be us timing love wrong?"

"No," He says, "We never did anything wrong. Love made the mistake, not us."

— E. Grin

"Why haven't you tried to talk to me?" He questions.

I give him a nearly silent sigh, trying to figure out an accurate way to form a sentence.

"Hmm?" He pushes.

I look down, and begin my sentences quietly.

"I want you happy," I tell, "but all I can seem to do is hold you back from living your life, and if my name doesn't fit in the same sentence as happiness, then I'll leave, because you don't deserve my negativity."

"But you need me," He says.

"I can tell myself that to make you stay, or I can tell us both the truth and say I can't be saved, not anymore."

"And what if I still decide to stay?"

I laugh, "I'd call you insane."

"Call me insane, then."

— E. Grin

Made in the USA
Middletown, DE
17 February 2017